The Oscillations

The Oscillations

Kate Fox

Nine
Arches
Press

The Oscillations
Kate Fox

ISBN: 978-1913437077
eISBN: 978-1913437084

Cover artwork: 'Winter Sea' © Spacefrog Designs.
www.spacefrogdesigns.com

First published February 2021 by:

Nine Arches Press
Unit 14, Sir Frank Whittle Business Centre,
Great Central Way, Rugby.
CV21 3XH
United Kingdom

www.ninearchespress.com

Nine Arches Press is supported using public funding by Arts Council England.

Supported using public funding by
ARTS COUNCIL
ENGLAND

Dedicated to all my fellow neurodivergent thinkers.

Here's to a more accepting world.

Contents

After

Pharmacopoeia

And suddenly the plagues
are the most interesting parts
of a city's history.

1635 stands out as the year
Yersinia Pestis took another tithe
from Amsterdam's population
and Doctor Tulp published his pharmacopoeia
to counter all the bad plague literature.

Later, he made a *Book of Monsters*,
wherein blacksmith Jan de Doot
sharpened his knife
and cut out his own bladder stone.

Tulp signed the fitness reports
for the first Manhattan settlers,
whose ancestors are still singing
Trip a Trap a Tronjes
(The father's knee is a throne)
four hundred years on –
the old rhyme meaning as much
or as little
as *Ring a Ring a Roses.*

I imagine a hotel bed,
two plane seats,
empty, waiting.

A space in front of 'Wheatfield with Crows',
where he will be overwhelmed by beauty
in a way I am trying to understand

while I brim with dark blue connective ribbons
obscuring, or highlighting,
the place where the path
meets the horizon.

13th March

One committed cougher
half way up the auditorium,
a sniveller in the front row
I couldn't get moved back
because the theatre said
seat reservations were pre-booked –

you almost in the corridor,
shadow across your face,
crying again at my story
of the swimmer
whose mother wouldn't let her
compete in the Olympics.

I didn't know I caught your eye,
me in the spotlight,
you in the dark,
how I woke you up.

You, constant as a mantel clock,
keeping track of the interval
and my fatigue,

seeing me as a Swiss watch
full of moving parts.

Overwhelmed now
by whatever entered us,
we have both stepped
out of time.

Stump

Like a punch from behind
a tooth breaking off at its bloody root
leaving you with a shocking black gap

like waking up at your own snore
gasping for air –

the upending of the world
when you put your foot
on a step that isn't there.

It's alright to tell us this had been
foreseen for years
in plans, models, rehearsals –

that's not how we were struck
that's not what froze our core
like the siren of the alarm clock
a white bomb glare.

So tell us again
about what always grows back

about slender shoots growing
from blasted stumps
green fishing rods into the future
tender rebuttals to the torn out page
that used to be tomorrow.

Here is destruction we can bear to look at.
Here is hope we can borrow.

The Distance i.

Anyone else get worried
watching people on telly
standing too close together,
they ask.

People want an explanation
of how quickly this distance
became their new lens.

We're wired to notice
what is dangerous
and therefore important.

I don't have a new instant overlay
for the world though, now spiky virus cells
circulate like planets.

I was always clumsy and elliptical,
unsure of the correct orbits

how close was too close,
how far too far.

I fix instead
on another left glove on a branch

singular as a vernal star.

The Distance ii.

We have come down from the fells
relieved how much longer
our breath lasts than a week before.
His text brings his daughters into the garden,
one onto a swing,
one onto a trampoline,
one telling me
she likes my hair.
His wife asks how I am,
I ask how she is,
with the new sincerity of these times.
She points out how much one of their girls,
who he currently cannot touch,
looks like him
and I agree,
even though most people
only look like themselves to me.
She hands me a sourdough starter in a Stork box
through the fence,
careful our fingers do not meet,
as far apart from us
as the registrar who made them laugh at their wedding.
She says it's seven days not fourteen
and he seems to agree.
I understand why you would listen
to someone who has raised humans
and bread, and worry I might struggle
to follow the rules for both.
Unsure if I am standing in the wrong place,
or the right one,

I separate from myself a little
as I cough into a bush on the path.
He warns me the hill back is steep
and thinking I cannot climb it
causes me to speed up,
scarf over my face, lungs cold,
until I have completed the impossible ascent
while yeast bubbles in my bag,
viral cells shed into countryside air
and people multiply like fear and rising loaves.

Skimming

The walk measured our breaths,
the first day
our knees ached going up the steps,
as we limboed under the tree
whose fall seemed to echo the world.

We sat on the stone beach
by the river, spectated the other side
as if it was a film.
How much movement there is
and sound, I said,
how quiet it is and still,
you replied.

A week later we will walk into the scene
and you will say change
is sometimes just a walk
on the opposite side of the river.

I am there now,
skimming stones uncertainly,
dunking them with a splash.
I had the knack once,
but needed to be re-taught
or un-learn the urge to throw.

My mother was not patient
about how clear I needed instructions to be,
how much longer than for other people
it takes me to learn by seeing,
or building up muscle memory.
Now I am quick to disguise
the ways in which I am slow.

So mercurial with words,
I couldn't learn the ways of your house alone.
There you are across the water.
Will you remember
how it really was,
when we found this place together?
Where did you go?

Cairns

Gathering flat stones from the sand
or bringing painted ones from home,
they hold their breath and balance
one on top of the other.

Here is a centre that holds,
patterns we can rely on,
things we make that might last
or keep us safe,
this pebble garden raised by hand,
contagious and unplanned.

Cairns, inukshuk,
waymarkers,
signs that we were here,
that we still are.

They walk among them hushed,
phones aloft,
as if these towers are the columns
in a cathedral.

Every day spreading further down the beach,
growing uncompetitively tall,
knocking together gently when they fall.

A message which says
in careful stacks of stone;
you are not alone,
you are not alone.

The Funerals

The funerals happened outside,
if at all, the end of that spring

when daffodil coronas crinkled
like elderly necks,
this year's tasks done,
lining the verges as if waiting for someone
to clear them away.

We gathered under the shelter
of the crematorium's porch,
semi-circling the coffin
they'd brought out on a trolley
like luggage.

A small music speaker,
a photograph of her magically restored
to twenty-two,
hand sanitiser in our bags,
seven shot glasses for sherry.

I didn't know the green globe
ready to release when the petals fall
is called an ovary.

Her neighbours placed a plastic folder
containing a photo collage of her garden
on the coffin.
The display she didn't get to see this year
had never been more magnificent

and something I only half-believed
when every afternoon ended
with the totting up of the dead –
the day after she died,
her daffodils bowed their heads.

The Choir

Outside there is a crosshatching of trees,
inside we are in separate boxes

but we are crossing over –
the singers, the exercisers, the talkers,
a delay of limbs blurring the screen,
only half-remembering we can be seen.

Somewhere, a blue garland of forget-me-nots
is shading a wall

while the choir talk about things
they are growing.

Parsley for the rabbit, cucamelons,
black opal basil, sunflowers, tomatoes.

Janet gets a round of applause
for having grown a grandson
from eggs she carried
when her daughter was inside her.

We plant our feet on the floor
to sing of trees in the heart of the forest

reaching for the sky,
how their roots go down dark and deep.

Our arms arc out of view
while the internet signal stutters and surges,

unpredictable as the conditions
that determine
which branches a tree
will be able to keep.

Returns

The plague books won't be in yet
but the dystopia section will be well-stocked
and you'd usually want two metres of space to browse anyway,
this last shop I came to on purpose, a pilgrimage.
Then, the assistant said they still had customers,
her son had been sent home for coughing in P.E.
So there's where I'll return first,
enjoy the full shelves, calming lines,
the glossy wooden lectern, the smell of new,
the rash of woodcut covers in striking monochromes,
the imprints from London, Chicago, New York.
I spent fifty pounds I no longer had last time, will spend another
fifty next, feeling I'm preserving an ecology, a sort of home.
So happy for this normality, my eyes will fill so the titles are blurred.
But reading? Reading, no. Can hardly take in a word.

Fret

A sea fret's rolling
towards the sealed-off telescopes.

We have only been able to look ahead
to the end of each day

but even this blurred version of a view
can show us something
we have never seen before.

Feel the sun cloched under clouds,
immerse yourself anyway.

Breathe

One, two, three
be mindful they say

if your epithelial cells
are under attack

just breathe

you can be whoever
you want to be, they say

despite the death of industry
expel the coal and metal dust
from your lungs

just breathe

we are all equal
we are all free, they say

even with a knee on your neck
just breathe

the sea and the trees
unclog in this pause

open to the sky

and just breathe
breathe
breathe

Possibility

After Jaan Kaplinski

If possibility is possible
then we could live a little beyond today
but not too far; a year is best, the General said,
avoid middle distances. In ultimatums and deadlines
lie disappointments. If possibility is possible
so is new weather, banana loaf,
another episode of the soap opera.
We may not sit blindfold on this rock
holding two crossed swords aloft,
but swim with gentle strokes
beyond the stone arms of the harbour
to where the car ferries and bulk carriers
glint static on the horizon
and follow the trail of the sun
like people who have remembered
they were once possible too.

Sea Swimmers

We used to go in twos and threes,
heads bowed, black-robed
like nuns on the way to matins.

Everybody sees we are curing ourselves
of something, but say only they could never face
the cold, that we are brave and mad.

We love to hear this, as much as they love
being allowed to say it.
The sky is usually iron and pewter now,

the water only a degree or two
colder than August.
We have to enter singly

under this week's rules,
layered in our obvious need,
forgetting the shock of immersion
again and again and again.

The Turning

If he does not want to shape time
with the pulling of a cracker,
raising of a glass

or stepping first into a house
I fear it will unspool into nothing
like that spring of Sundays.

But, as we scan the dark beach
for firework setters,
we both stop at what we still call

the Jojo Rabbit clock
where our eyes adjusted after cinema blackout
and a pink moon astonished the sky.

Explosions too far away to hear
are spraying colour into the grey,
clouds part on a moon just past full,

a face illuminated a minute after midnight
as if it is later that same day,
not a year on.

A stranger calls *Happy New Year, hope it's a better one*
from the other side of the pavement
and we marvel at how he really means it,

glance back at signal fires dotting the shore,
return through my door without noticing
which one of us is in front of the other.

Before

Raft

You see all the details at once
prompt me gently to read

the bright orange of the flotilla of life jackets
the light on the black shore
the men's reaching arms

until I see the pink inflatable ring
covered in Disney characters

and have to catch my breath
as it expands to fill my vision

the translation hits me at flashbulb speed
where others were tentative as the first words
in a new language I'm trying out loud

here is the girl who should have been playing
here is the girl this might not have saved
here is the girl who almost certainly survives.

Wet

Because, he says, some colours of oil paint
dry at different speeds –
when crimson is built up over lamp black say,
the black might take hundreds of years to dry,
still be wet in museums across the world –
isn't that amazing?
and I say, imagine you were standing
in front of it the day it dried,
you'd never know that was the exact day
the layers had finally separated,
isn't that amazing too?
We agree, both the staying wet
and the not knowing,

and us building up pictures with firm brushstrokes
until the layers bleed through
like thoughts looking for words.

Gormire Lake

An amphitheatre of dark green trees are an audience
that expect nothing from me.

A patrolling swan that can't be rescued from myth
without being trapped in another.

Soon I'll break the meniscus;
goosebump shoulders unreflected in the bottomless lake.

I'd love to dredge the black silt for genes
as they did with Loch Ness.

Eels, snakes, anthracite,
angry carpenter, emphysemic teacher,
trauma-damaged slug,
a prediction about the Adverse Childhood Experiences
of the damselfly.

The surface black and pixellated with white sparks,
a glider's horsefly drone.

A temporary ring as air and water meet
like a sentence begun and stopped.

German Girl

'German Girl' is a portrait by Euan Uglow and its banning from an Arts Council exhibition by Bradford Alderman Horace Hird made national and international papers in 1962.

A German Girl's hands are braced on her ham-thighs
as if she's about to plunge down a log flume.
She's got no clothes on, my Great Uncle
made them put her in a locked room
when the Arts Council brought her to Bradford in 1962.

She stares at me now on Google Images,
chin up, eyebrows slightly raised, basin of purposeful hair,
small dog ears of breasts pointing off to each side,
the brown triangle of her pubic hair the portrait's vanishing point.
Turns out she's actually Polish.

The archive shows Great Uncle Horace –
an owl in round black glasses –
hand resting on a gold mace embossed with boars,
Mayoral medallion warm on the centre of his chest,
ram and goat entwined in a disc of gold.

Pornographic, he said,
Lascivious.
It will corrupt families.
We don't want somebody to see it
and go off and do something unspeakable in the park.

His nephew married my mother
the year the Yorkshire Ripper started carrying a hammer
and women stopped walking on their own after dark.

My stepfather photographed me with no clothes on
each birthday from when I was four until I was eight,
straining to stand straight, arms at my sides, eyes front,
tiny, uncertain marble soldier.

My sister slowly puts the Polaroids
on a salvaged pile of childhood photographs
as if they're the winning cards in a game of snap,
another go down the log flume,
an unlocked room.

Shipley, West Yorkshire. 1981

Auntie Mary says it was the five pound note
she put in his wages that caught him in the end
but he was so clean, always so clean and polite,
one of their best drivers, which was why they bought him
a top-of-the-range truck, shiny wing mirrors, gleaming dash
and they were photographed in it together and it was framed
in the foyer at Clark's, him and her smiling, flash
glaring in the windscreen, her blonde bob and smile,
his neat black beard. Who knows where the photo is now.
The newspapers never got it, or the story, from Auntie Mary
and it's not her who tells that bit her sister-in-law always adds,
how journalists knocked on the door for months,
how her hair fell out and the blonde bob she has even now
is a wig. Shiny, straight hair other women
had given away   or sold.

The Forgetful

Searching my own filed words
as if they contain fingerprint clues
to the things my body knows.

Stored there; an archive of films
whose plots I have forgotten
whose character names I cannot recall
whose settings I cannot conjure
and whose reels have been
looping inside my skull
for years.

As I work to reconstruct the narratives
from fragments of script

my blood pumps unhesitatingly
to the rhythm of keys tapping *yes.*

My Parents as Cutlery

They took feeding seriously at first
though sometimes her sharp tines
dimpled a lip,
his serrated edge grazed a curious finger.
Judging distances is hard at first
and they made allowances

so it was a shock
like a stopped clock, the first time
You'll get what you're given
was spat on the formica like salt.

Her crown and his sceptre
once shone incandescent white
in the furnace of the forge
so we held them
loosely, took care not to cross them
on the blue speckled Denby.

Laid them down like amnestied weapons
on the proper pine table
While you're under our roof.
Secret chocolate wrappers rustled
and crumbed at the bottoms of all our bags.

Sometimes the scraping of the plates
sounded like a shriek and sometimes
like an orchestra improvised
by garden tools.

At Christmas there were mats
with crosshatch churches on,
cinnamon candles they'd brought back
from America,

all of us shining, burnished, full,
fairylights glowing in our chests
as we formed careful open-ended rectangles
like the ones we'd seen in films.

We carried the years carefully
in the bowls of our spoons.

The first photograph of his I saw that wasn't of me

No need to divine futures
between these scuffed stone walls
where repetition has always looked like prediction

and the labour of sun and soil and lifting
was something you could come and count in the night

where the boundary between out and in
was just a gentle reminder
in an acute triangle of effacing light

and you don't need to think
about what the door's reinforcing beams are for

and above the stepping-stone backs
of huffing cattle
a ladder is always leading into the dark

though even here, blinding light
looks like the future
a flash, bomb flare, a projector beam

as if the whole lot could lift
blades of hay, grain sacks eddying in the air

leaving a razed square of black grass
smoke rising at the edges.

Portrait

Something brave
in reading a person's light
to make a still
of their image
which captures them in flight.

Shell

And of course we've had the same dream
more than once, though maybe
people underestimate the likelihood
in the same way there's a fifty-fifty chance
you'll share the same birthday with someone else
in a room of twenty-three people.

This dream of driving fast with no lights on
(in my case there wasn't even a car)
just black road ribboning past like electricity down synapses
the unstoppable momentum

until my brain volunteered a solution
like the snake eating itself that explained DNA.

The whole: an egg held in a hand
speeded up like time-lapse film
breaking, white and yolk unfurling.

The fraction: a tiny turtle outline revealed
in the cracked shell.
The only possibility for growing;
one day at a time.

Masks

Here is a girl stood alone in the middle of a white aircraft hangar,
who needs somebody to take her hand,
here is a girl joyously kicking up brown leaves.

People mostly see only one of these.
Here is a girl wearing a badly-fitting clown mask
plastic mouth rim digging into her top lip

and a girl in a lacy blue body suit
which raises a red rash on her tummy.

Here is a girl who can make a room full of strangers
come to hug her like their own.

Here is a girl who doesn't quite recognise herself,
though there are always plenty of photos.

Here is a girl who became a woman
who can see behind masks and round corners
and hear the gaps between words and things
where light pours like falling water.

Here is a woman who knows
she can travel as fast as rewind
to where the girl stands alone
in a hangar filled with the sound
of arrivals and departures.

Here is a woman who knows
that it will never be too late to stand alongside
the girl in the hangar,
take hold of her hand and squeeze.

Asbestos

Because of how you nodded your head
and waited while I chased a thought
like a spaniel quartering to find the scent
of an animal it doesn't need to know the name of.
Because you said "Bright colours" when I walked in
and didn't really mean "Too bright".
Because you were a bricklayer first but didn't think
becoming a professor was a miraculous ascent.
Because when I said they had never served time as real buttons
you said "So they have exchange value, not use value"
and turned my neckwear into a Marxist statement.
Because, unlike the counsellor who said "Is that how you actually talk?",
you followed my sentences when they ran into each other,
like people moving stacks of chairs that are taller than they are.
Because of how when you came to hear my words, or read them,
your air moved through alveoli where those fibres were lying dormant
like facts learned for a history exam,
and your laugh resonated in the centre of my chest,
and from behind all anybody would have seen
were our shoulders shaking.

Scattering

You became a sudden grey shower,
a hoover bag bursting

when they sowed you like seeds
on the golf course.

Blew back gritty on their skin,
the skin your eggs set going.

An arc of you became every Benson & Hedges
you'd ever sucked in

with pursed lips, inhaling, inhaling
the shrunken wands that never filled you.

You'd scraped us off like crumbs of burnt toast,
dividing like your cells into good and bad,

not knowing how to answer when people asked
how many kids you had; "It was awkward".

You sloughed off relatives like the white powder
of callouses we pumiced from your feet,

the only times you let us touch you
as you lay shrinking, insensible, under white sheets.

You're not the trees left burned and broken
as pewter cairns on cold autumn mornings

but the man in that story who accidentally
trod a grass seed into the dust of a dead planet

then travelled thousands of years into the future
and gaped at savannah stretching to the carbonised horizon.

Things my mother said the last time we met

When I was little I had a tortoise called Timmy,
but one day he wasn't there.
My Dad said he got sent to live in Africa
which is a long way from Cleckheaton.
Your alarm clock was all I kept after you ran away.
I've still got it,
I'm not sure why I didn't get in touch
I was thinking about other things.
You know somebody tried to shoot your Dad
that day he got a puncture and had to go to the garage
then Jim tried to give him a heart attack
by putting something in his coffee.
Maybe I gave you too much independence
but it makes you stronger like that song *A Boy Named Sue,*
you've done alright anyway
since we last met was it – sixteen – years ago, haven't you?
The things you said
about your Dad and me going with those men
well, he's always seen himself as your Dad,
even if finding your birth certificate was a shock,
but you need to move on.
You always did have
a very vivid imagination.

Switch Off

She is ageing backwards,
soiled sheets and mattresses,
slopping about in shoes suddenly too big.

Money is doled out,
biscuits nibbled round the edges,
sentences repeated and repeated,
her hand must be taken down steps, crossing roads.

Before bed she crouches below the alcoves
where her Hummel figures pose
carefully turning off the switch to every plug
one by one.

Rosemary

Her neighbour says when he found her
on the bedroom floor
she thought she was in the playground in Baildon
and her Mum was coming to fetch her,
that I should try getting her to talk about the past.

I had been trying to stay
in the ever-shorter present
where an apartment in Mallorca still is,
sunrise over the sea
on Christmas Day,
one of the years we went away
so we didn't have to not belong
in a room of people with the same eyes,

where there's a photo on the telly stand
of our slide down into an Austrian salt mine,
the two of us laughing
as we sped down the polished wooden rail,
feet in the air like toddlers.

I have been avoiding knowing the Sunday
when me and her and my father
met for the first time,
has gone.

That day she said "I could write a book"
because of the seventeen years
I had only been imagined
and she rewrote every other story I'd been in –

about the illegitimate baby,
the standoffish girl,
the Runaway in the paper,
the Troubled Teen,
the Black Sheep, the Scapegoat
too clever for her own good –

to tell the one about Norman's daughter
she just clicked with straightaway,
who he was over the moon to meet,
the first story of me
that felt right,

but it has disappeared
along with her pillion rides up Baildon hills
on Norman's motorbike
when she was seventeen

and dancing in his arms to a big band
in the hall near the Alhambra

and the ashes she scattered in the daffodils
while I stood by one grey February day.

I can keep them though,
along with an image of a playground
where a dark moor is rising into the sky
and a girl is reaching out her arms
waiting for her mother to take her home.

What could be called communication

You might find them staying near the walls
or clutching their earphones,
rocking from foot to foot
and looking just above their audience.

They might be wincing at sirens,
saying *Pardon* a lot in crowds,
clutching the rails on angled walkways,
wondering at the calm faces of everybody else.

Sometimes they rest a foot on a crossed ankle
in such a way that others will click *Love*
in recognition when one of them
writes a Facebook post about it.

They might have coloured lenses
or squint perpetually into the sun.
They think everyone can see
the fluorescent lights humming.

Their eyes dart or fix
so they might be called evasive
or invasive.

They're stroking a finger,
twiddling with their hair,
tearing up paper, something
in a mesmerising rhythm.

They do not always recognise each other,
though are often to be found clustered
around tea urns,
outside where it's quiet

in the toilets at parties,
in wombs and rooms where everybody
shares the same nose
because of those contagious genes

so they can perpetuate their tangents
and straight lines,
build forests of themselves,

sending micellar releases of carbon and water
to those who need them,
survival tips, encouragement, warnings
in pulses of sound and light.

The stage

belongs to people who flicker
like early holograms,

who don't know who they are from one minute or month
to the next, and say things like
"I don't always agree with myself".

To people who can untangle the cat's cradle of invisible lines
between themselves and audience members in big coats.

To people who forget they can do this in black boxes
with bits of old masking tape and chalk marks on the floor

and stay entirely silent if they themselves are in the audience
and responses have been called for.

Who forget they can smooth the wires, illuminated by overhead gels,
into tracks between themselves and the people in the dark,

into the predictable forms of maps, photographs, memories
or a plan of a city grid at night,

seen from the air as if they were pilots descending,
stomach still feeling the fall after all this time.

Not Breaking the Egg

Bright blue, red, yellow
I can't stop looking
but then we have to cover it
with white wool

water and soap
turn and rub, press and mould round the egg
she says, you will feel
when it is felt.

The famous writer
tells us that my kind
only have feelings for ourselves.

I can't see how the colours
will get back on the outside,
will something dissolve?

I had told the front-row girl
with the rainbow fringe and eyebrows
they made me happy
and she flapped her hands at my prints
and how things matched.

It is cutting in the end –
scissors along the bottom
so the inside
becomes the outside,

more pressing and moulding,
relieved to be told
it's harder than you think
to break an uncooked egg.

Cetaceous

smooth and white
pouring yourself through me
I hear you hearing everything

strange beauty of your focused beam
which can tell the difference between
a gun pellet and a corn kernel
from sound echoing back fifty feet

triangulating data
scanning as you glide

your arcing leaps
your gentle, nosing joy

out of your element
you become useful to those
who say both that you are not like us
and that you are just like us
in a way that turns you shadow

but you make me fluid
as you navigate through the murk
with senses I didn't know existed
weaving sky into sea
sound into sight

you – I've said this before –
turning waves into light

The Navigators

Here is a paper chart of a city
on which you do not appear
and here is a blue dot on a screen that is not you or me.

A signal travels at the speed of light
positioning us relative to a satellite.

Our steps become more confident
as we check and recheck
each other's calculations and distances,
mindful of the gaps caused
by so much incoming information.

I look up how sextants work,
how two opposite mirrors superimpose
an image of the horizon and an image of a reflected star.

Discover how hard it is to measure angles quickly
how the earth always moves at fifteen degrees an hour
how there is always a need to know that this,
this now, is where we are.

From the heat, in the shadows

I am writing this on a fish
I will throw into the sea.
We are excited to discuss your latest metaphor
and how it might be translated into a language
that makes it beautiful.

Our blood runs warm as rain and thicker than you'd think.
We stand two feet too far from the microphone
at the comedy conference
which everybody points out is not funny,
and talk about you in a rising inflection.

Our toes point inwards,
a shaking hand wipes our brow,
we twist and untwist the lid of a water bottle
we will never drink.
We leave the stage saying quietly
"I've gone on for so long".

The question "Can you see a naked woman
and only laugh?"
follows us like the smell of last night's beer
until someone banishes it by asking:
"Is a male nude ever NOT funny?"

We are sorry about your small hands
and the failed revolution.
We are going back to basics.
You will find us taking classes in:
Awakening and Mercy,
Music and a Peaceful Soul,
Molotovs and Needlework.

You will find us *dhilal al hidaya*
(sheltering from the heat in the shadows),
consoling ourselves with the knowledge
that attitudes shift slowly
but we all shit and die.

You will find us on the deck of the boat
playful and wary as seals
until we flick our tails and dive,
become missiles parting the water
a roaring in our ears,
sure only of this velocity
and the unconcerned breadth of the ocean.

Notre Dame

A heat outside
great as the one inside
on days of making.

They fanned their wings frantically,
air conditioning their chosen future.

Experts in homeostasis,
living above a family of
grinning 13th century gargoyles.

Smoked to drowsiness,
gorging on honey.
It is only one long, wrong day

before figures in white
pick their way through fallen crosses,
stinking wet wood,
to carry sticky waxed cells from their home.

New dances will have to be learned,
new flowers found.

One hot day easier to recover from
than a century of fumes
hollowing out million-year-old limestone
until it collapses like untended honeycomb.

Rheology Two

Blood does not obey Newtonian rules either,
the flow changes depending on the stress applied –
same with paint, ketchup, your flow on my cheeks,
what was inside is outside,
what should be abjected is accepted onto skin,
my mask wipes clean. I am most myself when I swim.
Watching your golden arc into the dark of the sea
as if it is me, my liquefied limbs,
my bones lapse, I turn octopus, flushing pale or red,
squeezing myself through the gap of you
– or is it me, every tentacle decisive
with its own neurons,
as molten sun
staircases to the horizon.

The Fruits

He is not be allowed to be flesh.
When two white-coated women peered into the silver curves
and black shadows of the photograph made from sound,
they said he was the size of an apple pip.

When, according to the guides, he became blueberry
I knew I wanted to hold on to him until raspberry,
would have to let go before damson.

I googled descriptions week by week,
shutting down pictures with too much detail,
as if I'd strayed too far onto an ex's Facebook page.

Discovered he had eyelids,
nose, lips, but nobody could tell me
the exact point when his heartrate,
twice the speed of mine, would stop.

They slipped me two large round pills in silver packets,
I promised him I'd live,
surprised myself by accepting a sound-picture,
folding it carefully into my purse.

For weeks I passed chopped liver clots
which became red grapefruit, small melon
as if my body was shedding itself from the inside
to prove there was nobody there.

Maybe it would be okay to be Persephone after eating
the pomegranate seeds, spending half the year fucking
the Lord of the Underworld, half, watched over by a mother
who wanted me so much she killed the earth because I was gone,

or Pluto, prevented from boredom half the time
by missing the beloved who made his adrenaline run,
discovering he needed more of his own space than he realised
or the one I never could have thought – Ceres, gorged on love

deeper than eternal winter and full of loss as big as every crop
on earth, turning seeds over and over in her pocket
as she walks, finding ways to make those six months
pass over and over again.

Exile

and of course it felt like coming home,
we had both been exiled so long

but, told the ways of our country
were wrong,

I learned the customs of the new one
all too well,

they are drilled deep into women
so no one will be able to tell

we are not from here. Now, I don't belong
in our homeland any more

but fail to fit the new country too.
Your reflection of the gap between here and home

makes me feel close to you
and on my own.

Wolf Moon

Of course uncertainty makes us stock up for winter,
we are wasteful as wolves –

the huge yellow eye of the moon
stopped us at the promenade edge

when we couldn't speak after the film
flashed back to the mother's two-tone brogues,

the boy realising she was hanging from a lamppost.
How you choked on your words while we linked arms,

allowed an equivalent weight to unmoor in my stomach
like this moon into a cobalt sky,

how it halos between us now, soft as snow
covering a carcass under a tree.

Criminals had to pay debts in wolf tongues
not just because humans fear being torn apart

but because we recognise what it is
to believe you will never not be hungry

and lose yourself in a pack that runs and runs and runs
and is filled with blinding light.

Winter

The matchstick men are out on the Longsands again
so we wait until the sinister spire is completely black
against the aubergine sky,

say hello to the illuminated snowman at number thirty-seven,
whose lighting programme intermittently turns him gingerbread,

as we venture down to where dogs run along the waves,
their collar lights like tracer fire and claim this space as ours,

as if we have the right to be somewhere
without the clamour and buzz and accidental encounters
of days and streets.

We look for the fairy lights of the zombie trawlers
that have stuck to the horizon for months,

insulated by the chill from the people
who will be burning sausages and their own skin here
in a few months time.

Just us in thermal layers and wool over our ears
walking for once, into a scene we might have painted

of the hours before the crowds with icy breath gathered
for the unlocking of the factory gates.

Immersed

And the man who took my ring off said
"I would never go swimming with you
because you want to fight the sea,
I just want to look at it",

thinking I'd gone too far out
he would call me back over and over

until I washed up under a sea and a sky
as changeable as concrete in the rain,
to somebody who cannot swim
but shares a way to know

that searching for details
or making a bed or a plan or a story
are ways to stay as well as go –

arms braced,
buoyed by each other's breathing,

held as if there is only now
and the inexorable pull of the flow.

Emergency

Promenades and tables refilling
like the drip drip of the espresso machine

we look for normal
we look for calm
trying to forget even air
can cause us harm

and all the time
you were there
necessary and breathable

as parts of us kept emerging
like an arm out of a stuck sleeve
that big orange moon
the ferry beyond the pier
a snail after rain.

Both of us return again
through the emergencies
the snapped windscreen wiper
the laboured breaths
the last breaths
the torn muscle

while beneath us
between us
sometimes despite us
love spreads like a satellite signal
like sea foam
like spilt coffee on a counter top
like home.

Notes

Pharmacopeia: Doctor Nicolaes Tulp was a doctor who became Mayor of Amsterdam, partly because of the success of his books which included his *Pharmacopoeia* – a book of good medicines for chemists to prescribe. This was to counter all the ineffective medicines for Yersinia Pestis – the Black Death – which flooded the market in Amsterdam's bad plague year in 1635. Thanks to Philip Rush and David Harmer for our virtual trip to Amsterdam which inspired this poem, and Colin for the real one.

The Stump, Cairns, The Funerals, The Choir, Fret and **Breathe** were written as part of my 'Twelve Days of Lockdown' project, a commission from Unlimited, in which me and photographer Colin Potsig collaborated on poem-videos inspired by our lockdown walks.

The Turning and **Wolf Moon** both refer to Taika Waititi's comedy-drama film *Jojo Rabbit,* about a boy's absurdist response to growing up in Nazi Germany.

Raft was inspired by a photograph from Ivor Prickett's exhibition about the battle against Isis in Iraq and Syria, 'End of the Caliphate', on at the Side Gallery in 2019.

Shipley, West Yorkshire, 1981 refers to Peter Sutcliffe, the serial killer known as the Yorkshire Ripper.

Asbestos is in memory of Professor Calvin Taylor, my PhD supervisor, who died of mesothelioma in 2018.

Rosemary is in memory of my stepmum Rosemary Reynard who died of Vascular Dementia and, possibly Covid 19 (she was never tested) in April 2020.

What could be called communication draws a parallel between neurodivergent people and the recently discovered knowledge – for example, see Peter Wohlleben's *The Hidden Life of Trees* – that trees communicate using their root networks.

Many of the poems in this collection touch on neurodiversity – the idea that, as in biodiversity, there is a strength in the difference of people with conditions such as autism and ADHD who think and experience the world differently. Particularly – 'The Distance i.', 'Skimming', 'The Turning', 'Raft', 'Masks', 'The Stage', 'Not Breaking the Egg', 'Cetaceous', 'The Navigators', 'Exile' and 'Immersed'.

Recent social scientific research is examining the idea that many fewer women than men are diagnosed with these conditions because they are socialised to mask or camouflage their differences. (For example, see the work of Will Mandy. For the perspectives of autistic and ADHD adults I would particularly recommend the Twitter hashtags #actuallyautistic and #adhdsquad as starting points.)

I would love to name the famous writer in **Not Breaking the Egg** here, but I'm not going to...

Thanks and Acknowledgements

I would like to give general acknowledgement to Peter and Ann Sansom's wonderful Poetry Business Advanced Course and all its participants. Particularly my lockdown groups of Philip Rush and David Harmer, and Amanda Dalton and Cheryl Moskowitz.

I would also like to thank my fellow autistic writers and speaker-outers for constant inspiration and support – particularly the lockdown threaders Sonia Boue, Laura James, Joanne Limburg and Katherine May.

The time since March 2020 has been a time of both chaos and healing. I've felt lucky to be grounded by the sea in Whitley Bay and to have had the support of excellent beings both near and far, particularly: Colin and Willow, the Sea Gals, Helen and Sharon, Julia, Abigail, Astrid and Polly, Su, Jill, Karen, and Sarah.

My life was also much improved by the lattes and pastries of Cullercoats Coffee, The Boatyard in Cullercoats, Gareth James Chocolatiers in Tynemouth, Castle Bakery in Morpeth's deliveries and Pure Knead and Kith and Kin in Whitley Bay. I did do other things than go on walks with lattes in the middle of them, honest. Including write many of the poems in this book – and huge thanks go to Jane Commane for her wonderful editing, and all at Nine Arches. I've never felt more grateful to small indie businesses of all kinds.